W9-ABY-466

Games for Global Awareness

by
Jan Asch

illustrated by Becky Radtke

Cover by Kathryn R. Marlin

Copyright © 1994, Good Apple

Good Apple
1204 Buchanan St., Box 299
Carthage, IL 62321-0299

All rights reserved. Printed in the United States of America.

Paramount Publishing

NO LONGER THE PROPERTY
OF THE
UNIVERSITY OF R.I. LIBRARY

UNIVERSITY OF RHODE ISLAND LIBRARY

Copyright © 1994, Good Apple

ISBN No. 0-86653-792-9

Printing No. 98765432

Good Apple
1204 Buchanan St., Box 299
Carthage, IL 62321-0299

The purchase of this book entitles the buyer to reproduce the student activity pages for classroom use only. Any other use requires written permission from Good Apple.

All rights reserved. Printed in the United States of America.

For lovers and haters of geography everywhere, but especially for Frank and Devin, my favorite players.

Copyright © 1994, Good Apple

GA1486

Contents

Copyright © 1994, Good Apple

GA1486

Index of Maps and Flags

Copyright © 1994, Good Apple

GA1486

Introduction

"Our woeful ignorance and lack of curiosity about the world beyond our borders amount almost to a national character flaw. Part of the reason is the short shrift given by our schools to geography."

Alex Shoumatoff
Author of *The World Is Burning*

The only thing I remember about studying geography in elementary school was the neat roll-down map at the front of the classroom and my disappointment at how infrequently we used it. At home, on the other hand, I recall a wooden puzzle map of the United States that I never got tired of. But mostly, I remember playing "Geography" with my family on long car trips. Looking back I realize that as a child I had a natural love of geography. I think all children do. So why don't our schools take advantage of this natural inclination? The answer might be the belief that geography is boring–too much dumb stuff to memorize. And, there just isn't time; after all, geography is only a small part of social studies.

If this sounds all too familiar, maybe this book can be of help. Using games to teach children is nothing new. In every culture known to humankind children have been taught adult skills by means of games–games children have invented themselves or games that were handed down from generation to generation. If something is fun, kids are the first ones to notice. If presented in the right spirit, games are nonthreatening. Games are the enemy of boredom, and yet they invite repetition.

The games and activities in this book encompass many different learning styles and levels of skill. Teachers using a thematic approach are sure to find a match for just about every need. Home-schooling parents or civic group leaders will also find it a flexible and invaluable tool.

Whether you're using this book to help plan a six-week unit, or just browsing for a couple of good games to keep the kids quiet in the car, be forewarned: playing geography games can be habit-forming!

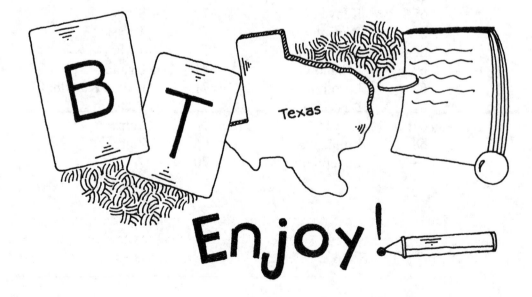

Copyright © 1994, Good Apple

GA1486

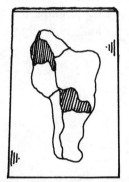

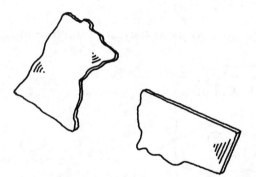

Map Games

No learning environment should be without globes, simple wooden puzzle maps, and jumbo cardboard jigsaw puzzle maps. Kids love them, and they are among the few geography materials that are readily available these days. Here are a few games and activities that will expand their use.

Copyright © 1994, Good Apple

GA1486

The Globe Game

Materials:

globe
blindfold (or just ask players to keep their eyes closed)

Players:

two or more

Procedure:

Blindfold the first player and give the globe a spin. The blindfolded player puts one finger on the globe to stop its spinning and tries to answer the following series of questions without removing the blindfold, scoring one point for each correct answer.

1. Are you in the northern or southern hemisphere? (Almost everyone scores a point here if the concept has been presented.)

2. Are you on land or water?

3. If you are on land, what continent do you think you have landed on? If you are on water, what ocean?

4. If you are on a continent, what country do you think you have landed on?

Playing this simple game increases awareness of all the players as they are forced to look at the globe in more and more detail.

Copyright © 1994, Good Apple

2

GA1486

Crash Landing

Materials:

two globes

Players:

two

Procedure:

One player pretends to be a space shuttle astronaut that has crash-landed somewhere on the earth. The other pretends to work at Houston Control to locate and rescue the astronaut. The astronaut spins the globe and puts a finger on it to stop its spinning and to put the players in a random place on the globe. Houston Control asks questions similar to those on page 2 to try to determine as nearly as possible the location of the crashed astronaut. When Houston Control believes there is enough information, it says "Help is on the way to . . . (the location)." If this is incorrect, the astronaut radios the position again, only this time more precisely, until Houston Control is able to rescue the shuttle.

Variations:

This game can be used to learn latitude and longitude. The astronaut radios in the position, giving the latitude and longitude. Houston Control must figure out the location.

Copyright © 1994, Good Apple

3

GA1486

Map Matching Game

Materials:

wooden, cardboard, or other puzzle map
poster board
marker

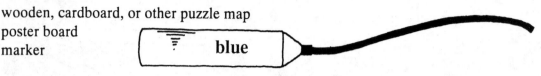

After players have become familiar with a group of continents by shape, it is possible to create a simple matching game with the names of the continents, countries, states, or provinces.

Players:

two

Preparation:

Trace all of the puzzle pieces on a separate piece of poster board. At the bottom of each card write the name of the continent or country. For this stage of the game you need not make a separate set of name cards, but you may if you like. Try to mark the puzzle pieces and the backs of the cards with corresponding color dots or some other form of identification for controlling errors. This way, if the children are working alone, they will know if they have the right answers. Put both the puzzle pieces and the cards on a tray and store them on a shelf where children can choose this activity on their own.

Presentation:

When presenting this material to the children, be sure to show them the dots on the reverse sides of the puzzle pieces and cards. Also repeat the names of the continents or countries as you match each puzzle piece and card. Children who can't read but know initial sounds will often be able to guess the right names of the countries. The use of the cards is also a visual recognition exercise for long words, practice which can be very useful later as an adjunct to sight reading.

Variations:

Put one set of matching pieces far away from the other and ask the player to "go get the Africa piece," showing him or her the shape on the empty card.

South America

Copyright © 1994, Good Apple

4

GA1486

Map Templates

Materials:

poster board, bristol board, thin cardboard, or stencil acetate
X-acto™ knife
colored pencils
paper cut to size of template

Preparation:

Trace the map outlines of continents, nations, states, or provinces onto heavy poster board or acetate and cut the shapes out with an X-acto™ knife. Place the cutout shape on a tray or work area with colored pencils and paper cut to fit the template. Place a black dot or some other symbol at the top left of the template so the child will know which end goes up.

Presentation:

Demonstrate how to trace the outline of the country. Be sure to point out the black dot or symbol used to mark the top.

Variations:

1. Ask a player to try drawing with closed eyes.

2. Have someone put a finger on one of the insets. Can the person guess which one it is by tracing it with his or her finger?

3. Make folders for the countries that go together (for example: all the countries of South America). Label and color them.

4. Try copying simple outline maps freehand. You can construct the entire world this way.

5. Decorate your maps with physical features, people according to population, languages spoken (color codes), or famous landmarks.

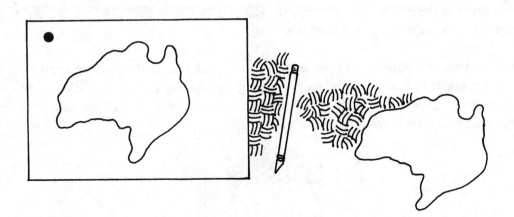

Copyright © 1994, Good Apple

GA1486

Blind Man's Bag

Materials:

cloth bag, box, hat, or basket
puzzle map
blindfold (or just ask players to keep their eyes closed)

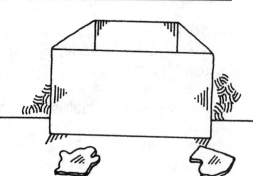

Players:

This game may be played by one, two, or more players.

Procedure:

Place the puzzle pieces into the bag (a box, hat, or basket will do fine also) and mix. With eyes closed, the first player draws a piece and tries to name the continent, state, or province simply by feeling its shape. If the player guesses correctly, he or she puts the puzzle piece down and takes another turn. If the guess was incorrect, the player must place the puzzle piece back in the bag and the next player gets a turn. Play continues until all the pieces have been drawn and guessed correctly. At the end of the game, each player counts his or her number of correct guesses to determine the winner.

Variations:

1. A cooperative version of this game can be played by proceeding in the same manner as above but having the goal be to identify all of the pieces regardless of who guesses correctly. Since incorrect guesses will be replaced in the bag, players will learn by their mistakes and eventually be able to get them all.

2. A solitaire version of this game can be played and is an excellent way to reinforce map skills.

3. For beginners, or those with limited knowledge of the pieces, start with four or five pieces (two or three pieces for children under the age of five). Before putting the pieces in the bag, show them to the children and say their names. "This is Africa. This is North America. This is South America." Next, ask the children to identify them. "Show me South America. Show me North America. Show me Africa." Finally, pointing to each piece, ask the children to repeat the names by asking, "What is this?" After correct responses have been given for each of the puzzle pieces, ask the children to close their eyes and feel each piece before placing it in the bag and proceeding with the game as above.

4. This version is for two players only. Instead of using a bag, the first player chooses a piece for his or her opponent to guess. The player who is guessing must keep eyes closed, of course. Play continues as above. The strategy involved in choosing the "right" piece for your opponent to guess makes this version very interesting.

Copyright © 1994, Good Apple

GA1486

Put puzzle pieces into the basket (bag, box, etc.).

Then... Player needs to keep eyes closed and pick a puzzle piece. Can the player guess what it is by the shape?

Help beginners by showing and naming puzzle pieces before the game starts.

South America

And this is South America.

Copyright © 1994, Good Apple

GA1486

Cut 'n' Guess

Materials:

paper
scissors
map of United States or others

Players:

two or more

Procedure:

One person looks at the map and chooses a state or province without telling which one it is. Then he or she takes a piece of paper (reused or recycled paper, please!) and begins to cut out the shape of one of the states or provinces. The other participants try to guess which state or province it is. For beginners it is helpful to have maps available for both cutters and guessers. Whoever guesses correctly first gets the scissors next.

Variations:

1. See how many states or provinces you can get out of one piece of paper.

2. When your kids get good at it, try doing it without the maps. Not everyone will be able to think of a state or province whose shape can be easily cut, so you may want to let whoever has one try to stump his or her classmates next.

3. Save your cuttings and make a collage.

4. Play successive games with no repeats until you have done all the states or provinces. Paste them together in a map collage.

5. For team play: One person is the cutter for the entire game. He or she must choose states or provinces at random to cut. Two teams guess simultaneously. The states or provinces are pasted in columns for the teams that guess them. The team with the most guesses at the end of the game wins.

Copyright © 1994, Good Apple

GA1486

Maps of Familiar Places

Making maps of familiar places can be a wonderful way for children to grasp what maps are all about. Consider asking the kids to make their own personal maps, or collaborate and do a group map.

Work Large:

If you are making a map of your town, it's fun to work in a large format. Illustrate the map with drawings, photographs, or postcards of famous landmarks and prominent buildings. End rolls of good quality paper are usually available free at your local press and make good maps.

Work Small:

Each individual can create a map of the same place. It is amazing to see how each map will differ.

Go 3-D:

Papier-mâché or clay works well, especially if you want to include physical features of your state or province. Dioramas are an excellent format for maps of indoor areas. Sculpey or Fimo clay comes in many colors and can be fired safely in your oven at home.

Suggestions:

Your learning environment; a child's room at home; your street; your neighborhood; the way to your school; a floor plan of your house; your state or province; famous sites such as the Grand Canyon, Mt. St. Helens volcano, the pyramids in Egypt; Paris with a view of the Eiffel Tower; the Great Wall of China; a tropical rain forest; a city skyline; or hands-on illustrations of simple physical features such as islands, lakes, mountains, valleys, plateaus, glaciers, river deltas, peninsulas, gulfs, etc.

Variations:

1. Contrast maps showing the development of an area over a long period of time (for example, primitive to modern)

2. Contrast 3-D maps showing the difference between a desert culture and an arctic one, a rural settlement and an industrial one

Copyright © 1994, Good Apple

GA1486

Basic Orientation

Materials:

blindfold (optional)
directions

Players:

two or more, or teams

Preparation:

Write out directions on a few small pieces of paper and give one to the player without the blindfold.

Procedure:

Blindfold one player and have him or her walk five steps to the north, three steps to the south, one step east, and nine steps west (or any combination of the above) and guess the location. Then switch and let a partner have a turn with the blindfold. If players are not yet familiar with the directions north, south, east, west, you can use left, right, straight, back.

Variations:

1. Using a familiar trip (for example, to the bathroom), have players count the steps to the north, south, etc., and write them down. Children will have fun cataloging different "trips." It is a wonderful way to introduce a discussion of navigational techniques.

2. Using a giant map of a country, try the above having the blindfolded player guess where he or she is.

Copyright © 1994, Good Apple

GA1486

What's Missing?

Materials:
tray
cloth big enough to cover tray
puzzle map pieces

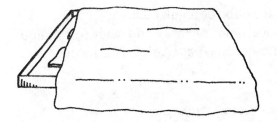

Players:
two or more

Procedure:
Show the group the pieces on the tray. Name them. Then remove one piece where no one can see you. Replace the cover. Let one of the children take off the cover and try to guess which piece is missing.

Note:
The degree of difficulty can be controlled by adding or subtracting from the number of pieces on the tray or by the amount of time allowed for viewing the objects.

Variation:
Which One Doesn't Belong? Played the same as above except that all of the puzzle pieces but one are from the same continent or country. Players have a limited time (while the cover is off) to identify which piece is wrong.

Copyright © 1994, Good Apple

GA1486

Around the World

Materials:

colored cube or regular die

political map of the world with (or without) names of countries and continents outlined and color-coded (Asia, Africa, North America, South America, Europe, and Oceania)

Players:

two or more, or teams

Preparation:

Use a die or a cube with a different color on each side: red, yellow, orange, green, blue, purple. Let each color or each number on a die stand for one of the continents. For example, Asia = 6, Africa = 5, North America = 4, South America = 3, Europe = 2, Oceania = 1. A reproducible score sheet grid is shown on the opposite page.

Procedure:

The first player rolls the die, and if the number 6 comes up (corresponding to Asia), the player must find a country in Asia on the map and write (or the teacher may write) its name on the score sheet under the Asia column. The next player does the same. Play continues until one player has filled three sections of the score sheet grid, meaning three of the following: 6 African nations, 5 European, 4 Asian, 3 South American, 2 North American, and 1 from Oceania. If a player rolls a number for which the existing blanks have already been filled, he or she must pass the die to the next player. (The numbers should be switched around from time to time to make play more challenging, as players will begin to name the same two or three countries from a place over and over.)

Variations:

More advanced players can try playing without a map or with a map that does not have the names of the countries written on it. After rolling the die, the player must name a country from that continent and fill in the score sheet grid as above.

Copyright © 1994, Good Apple

GA1486

Around the World Score Sheet

Player:	Player:
Africa	**Africa**
1	1
2	2
3	3
4	4
5	5
6	6
Asia	**Asia**
1	1
2	2
3	3
4	4
5	5
Europe	**Europe**
1	1
2	2
3	3
4	4
South America	**South America**
1	1
2	2
3	3
North America	**North America**
1	1
2	2
Oceania	**Oceania**
1	1

Copyright © 1994, Good Apple

GA1486

Blindfolded Journey

Materials:
blindfold
pencil or marker
map (can be played standing up with a giant classroom-sized map or individually with photo-
copied maps)

Players:
two

Procedure:

The first player puts on the blindfold. The second player guides a pencil to the starting place (perhaps the player's home state if working with a United States map). "Now you are in Maine," he or she says. "See if you can get to Texas." The blindfolded player tries to visualize the map and draws a line to where he or she thinks Texas would be. When the game stops, the player takes off the blindfold and sees where he or she ended up.

Variation:

1. As the blindfolded player goes over each state or country, the other player says, "Now you're in New York. Now you're in Pennsylvania. . . ."

2. Hints can be given, such as "You're getting hotter. . .you're getting colder."

3. Instead of a specified destination, the second player may say, "Now you're in Maine. Okay, now go south. Now go north. Good. Now go west. Okay, where are you?"

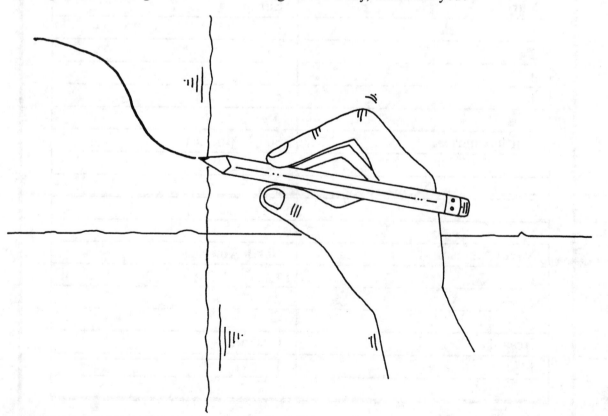

Copyright © 1994, Good Apple

14

GA1486

Guessing Games

In this section you will find a variety of guessing games. Some require little in the way of materials and are thus suitable for playing in the car or in the bus on the way to a field trip. Others lend themselves to large groups or team play. Or maybe you'd like to try your hand at making up your own place riddles and geograms.

Copyright © 1994, Good Apple

GA1486

Alphabet Soup

Materials:

basket or hat
alphabet cards
timer
pads of paper
pencils

Players:

two or more, or teams

Preparation:

Make a small card for each letter of the alphabet (except *x, z* and any other letters you think would be discouraging). Put them in a hat or basket.

Procedure:

One player chooses a card without looking. In a limited time, say thirty seconds, both players or teams have to think of geographical locations that begin with that letter and write them down. Spelling doesn't count. Compare the lists. Cross out any that are the same. Players or teams score one point for each original answer they have on their lists. First to score 25 points wins the game. If you draw the same letter twice, replace it and draw another. Double letters score two points (for example, Point Pleasant).

Variations:

1. In preparation for this game, you may want to see how many geographical locations the students can name as a group beginning with the letters *a, b, c*, etc., and list them on the board.

2. See how many one-syllable, then two-syllable, then three-syllable, etc., geographic locations you can name that begin with each letter.

3. You may limit your locations to certain continents, countries, or even to other things like cities, capitals, rivers, mountains, or lakes.

Alaska, Africa and Alabama—that makes 25 points! I win!

Copyright © 1994, Good Apple

GA1486

Geography

Materials:

Players:

two or more

Preparation:

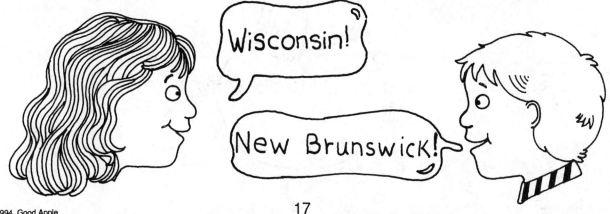

Procedure:

One person names a geographic location. The next player must think of one that begins with the letter the last player's location ended with. For example, if the first player says Vermont, the second player must say a place that begins with the letter *T*, like Texas. The third player must think of a place that begins with the letter *S*, like Scotland. And so on. No place name may be repeated, so even if there are two places called Rome (the one in Italy and the one in New York), only one is permissible. Decide ahead of time if you will allow bodies of water and mountains. Omit words like *the* or *an* when determining what letter you have, so that The Galapagos would be considered a *G*. Some rules do not permit using words like *Islands, River,* or *Mountains.* So instead of saying Hudson River you'd just say the Hudson. But you can invent your own "house" rules.

If a player can't think of a place for the letter, he or she is out. The next player, however, must take that letter. When all the players have been eliminated except two, the remaining player must think of a place beginning with the letter that stumped his or her opponent to win the game.

Variation:

Setting a time limit for answers keeps things from getting dull in this game. You can also even things up by giving better players less time to guess.

Suggestions:

You will soon discover that a lot of the countries that begin with *A* end with *A*, or that many places end in *E*. Whenever I play, especially with children, I make it a point never to say a location that begins and ends with *A*. That way at least children hear lots of other *A*s that they will begin to use themselves. Look in an atlas and make a list of place names together that they can use in difficult situations (like *A*s, *E*s, *X*s, and *Z*s).

Copyright © 1994, Good Apple

17

GA1486

Snowman

This game is based on the popular game Hangman but renamed for those who find violent images offensive.

Materials:

flannel board or chalkboard
three white circles, black hat, orange carrot nose, red scarf (or any combination of eyes, mouth parts, etc.)

Players:

two or more

Procedure:

Think of a geographic location. Young players who may not be good spellers may choose the name out of a hat. Write a blank for each letter in the name. Players randomly choose letters of the alphabet to fill in the blanks. If they choose a correct letter, fill it in where it goes in the blanks. If they miss a letter, draw a circle on the chalkboard, or place one of the pieces of the snowman on your flannel board. You may vary the difficulty of the game by the number of misses allowed. For example, you can have a snowman made up of only head, middle, and base. The head can already be decorated with eyes, nose, and hat. Or you can give him eyes, nose, mouth, hat, arms, buttons, etc., as part of the game. A list of the letters incorrectly guessed should be visible to all. If someone repeats an incorrect letter, he or she may try again.

Variations:

1. Team play. One team guesses until they miss a letter. Then it is the other team's turn. The first team to guess the answer wins.

2. Limit your game to geographic locations in the United States or Africa, for example. Players may pass without penalty.

Copyright © 1994, Good Apple

GA1486

Who Am I?

Here is another classic. This game is similar to Twenty Questions, only there is no limit to the number of guesses a person can make.

Materials:

Players:

two or more

Procedure:

The first player thinks of a geographic location. The other players ask questions about this place which require only a yes or no answer. For example:

"Are you in the northern hemisphere?"
"Yes."
"Are you in Asia?"
"No."
"Are you in Europe?"
"Yes."
"Are you a country?"
"Yes.
"Do your people speak French?"
"No."
"Are you bordered by water?"
"Yes."
"Is your capital Rome?"
"No."
"Are you known for your tulips?"
"Yes."
"Are you Holland?"
"Yes!"

The person who guesses correctly gets to think of the next place.

Variation:

This format can also be used for flags (see Flag Games) or other specific things.

Copyright © 1994, Good Apple

GA1486

Capital Riddles

Here is a list of challenging riddles for guessing capital cities. Try making up some of your own. It's fun.

Suggestions:

Start your social studies class off right with a riddle a day! Or better yet, let the kids make up their own. Type them out and pass them on! Here are some capital riddles, but you can make up riddles for any place names.

Riddles:

1. I may not know this capital, but for sure *you* do.

2. I'm no Rock of Gibraltar.

3. I am very religious peppermint candy.

4. I am a month, a wind.

5. I am French for Peter.

6. I am a wealthy baseball pitcher's place.

7. You work for me and I weigh 2000 pounds.

8. I am a timid girl's name.

9. I've seen it all, but mostly I've seen wars.

10. Ring me, but do it quickly!

11. I am what fires do.

12. I am a university in Washington, D.C.

13. I am a type of bean.

14. The most recent sandwich shop

15. To wander

Answers:

1. Juneau (Alaska) 2. Little Rock (Arkansas) 3. Sacramento (California) 4. Augusta (Maine) 5. Pierre (South Dakota) 6. Richmond (Virginia) 7. Boston (Massachusetts) 8. Cheyenne (Wyoming) 9. Warsaw (Poland) 10. Belfast (Northern Ireland) 11. Bern (Switzerland) 12. Georgetown (Guyana) 13. Lima (Peru) 14. New Delhi (India) 15. Rome (Italy)

Copyright © 1994, Good Apple

GA1486

Geograms

Geograms are illustrated clues for place names. Sometimes they are called rebuses. Try these; then try making up your own.

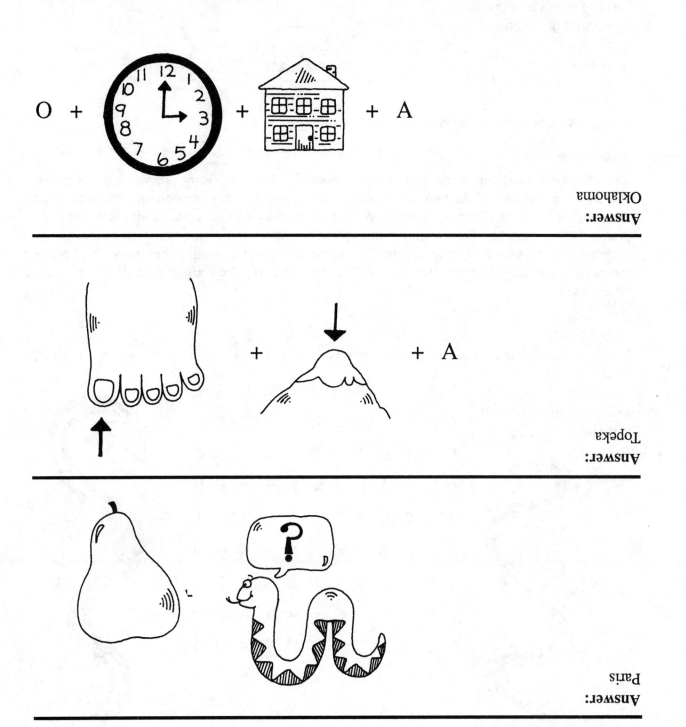

Answer: Oklahoma

Answer: Topeka

Answer: Paris

Copyright © 1994, Good Apple

21

GA1486

Geowordfind

Materials:

two hats
two copies of Geowordfind
two copies of countries list
photocopier
scissors

Players:

This game is most fun if played by two teams.

Procedure:

The following word search has geographical words hidden in it. Some are vertical, some horizontal, some diagonal. Make two copies of the word search and put them on opposite sides of the room out of the view of the contestants. Write each country on two separate sheets of paper and put one set in each hat. Each team member picks a country out of the hat, crosses the room to where the word search is hung and tries to locate the place chosen. When successful, player returns to the start and the next person may choose a country. The team to find all of their words first wins.

Suggestion:

You can make your own word searches based on the states or countries that you are currently studying. These word finds can be for individual use in folders or for team play.

```
P  S  W  B  R  A  Z  I  L  D  G  L
K  A  T  I  T  D  R  I  G  E  E  K
I  U  T  M  T  G  D  T  E  N  R  C
K  D  P  A  N  A  M  A  R  F  E  H
H  I  S  E  Y  Y  L  A  M  I  G  I
Y  A  S  S  J  K  N  Y  A  N  G  N
U  R  I  T  M  I  W  S  N  T  F  A
T  A  U  E  F  E  E  A  Y  A  I  N
F  B  G  S  D  K  E  N  Y  A  N  D
D  I  D  R  S  P  A  I  N  L  S  F
Z  A  F  A  F  I  Y  N  K  Y  P  N
C  C  A  N  A  D  A  A  L  G  E  R
```

| Canada | Kenya | China | Germany | Brazil |
| Italy | Panama | Russia | Spain | Saudi Arabia |

Copyright © 1994, Good Apple

22

GA1486

Copyright © 1994, Good Apple

23

GA1486

Spot the States

Materials:

notebook
pencil

Players:

two or more

Procedure:

A running list of the license plates spotted and their states or provinces are kept in a notebook. The idea is to see how long it takes to get all fifty states or ten provinces. Interstate highways and large tourist attraction parking lots are prime locations. This game can be played cooperatively, where each person in the car adds to a single list, or competitively, where the states or provinces spotted are tallied and someone is declared the winner for the day, trip, or as the first one to spot all the states. Both versions are fun.

Copyright © 1994, Good Apple

GA1486

Boast

Boast is a guessing game my husband made up in the car recently on our way to the beach.

Materials:

paper
pencils (optional)

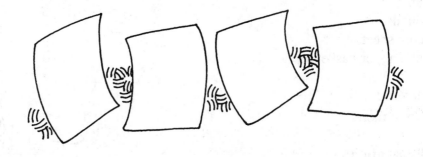

Players:

two or more

Procedure:

The first player boasts: "I can name five places that start with the letter *M*. The second player counters, "I can name six." (The players must either bid higher with the same letter, challenge the first boast, or pass. If they pass, the bidding passes to the next player. If the high bidder is challenged, he or she lists the six countries that begin with the letter bid. If successful, award six points (one for each). If the bidder fails to do so, the person who challenged gets all the points even if five were named successfully. If no one challenges, no points can be awarded and round two begins. The person to the left of the one who won the bid last bids first in the next round. If you wish, you may set a time limit. Play continues until someone has a total of 25 points. Or if it's more convenient, the player with the most points when you get there wins.

Variations:

1. The first bidder can vary the category from round to round (but not within the round). The first player says: "I can name three rivers that begin with *M*. He or she is challenged successfully. In the second round the first bidder may say, "I can name three capitals that begin with *T*". . . . In the third round the first bidder may say, "I can name four continents that begin with *A*." "Brilliant strategy!" you think, but since everyone knows there are only four continents that begin with *A* everyone passes and no one scores.

2. Instead of naming the places beginning with a letter, apply a different constraint. For example, the first bidder would say, "I can name seven states that border the Atlantic Ocean," or "I can name ten of the provinces of Canada." Play continues as above. Some suggestions for this variation are:

Cities in the United States
Mountains
Spanish-speaking countries
Countries that have a cross on their flag
Nations that are not part of the U.N.
States that share a border with Canada
Places that have only one syllable
Places that were named for famous people
Places that have Native American names
Places that begin with *A* but don't end in *A*
Places whose capital city has the same name
Cities that are located on the coast

Copyright © 1994, Good Apple

25

GA1486

Place Pictures

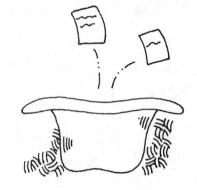

Materials:

paper
pencils
score sheet
hat, bag, or basket (optional)

Players:

two or more

Preparation:

Write the names of a few geographic locations on separate pieces of paper and put them in a hat.

Procedure:

Players or teams pick one of the names, and in a specified time draw a picture that will help the teams guess the geographic location on their paper. Letters, numbers, and symbols (+, ÷, -, x, etc.) are not permitted.

Suggestion:

Use rhymes (*sounds like* can be symbolized by a picture of an ear), pictures of famous tourist attractions (Eiffel Tower), or draw an outline map of the place and put an arrow showing the location of the place on your paper.

Copyright © 1994, Good Apple

GA1486

Flag Games

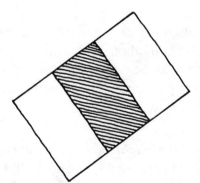 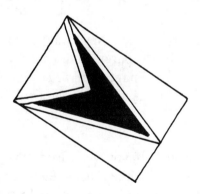

Using flags is one of the most powerful ways of attracting kids to geography. Flags are colorful, varied, plentiful, and aesthetically pleasing. Unfortunately, because of the expense of full color reproduction, I can only offer you suggestions for creating your own flag cards. The games presented are some of the many ways flags can be used in your learning environment.

Copyright © 1994, Good Apple

GA1486

Flag Cards

Here are some suggestions for making flag cards. It is a lot of work, but when you consider how much kids love flags, it's worth it. Commercial sets are hard to find, can be prohibitively expensive, and are usually out-of-date. The flag outlines in the Appendix can be increased in size with most photocopy machines or enlarged with overhead projectors and traced for making poster-sized flags. Correct colors can be added by consulting a recent almanac. You'll note some flags have the same overall design but with different colors and symbols. Information for obtaining complete sets of the flags is also available in the Appendix.

Materials:
3" x 5" (7.62 x 12.7 cm) index cards for making small cards, or paper or poster board for making large flags
pencils
markers or poster paint
overhead projector or tracing paper
copy machine that can make reductions and enlargements
flag poster, flags from almanacs, U.N. postcards, games, stickers, etc.

Suggestions:
Have each person in the group be responsible for making one or more flags. Ask parents to volunteer their help in making or donating needed materials.

Method 1: The easiest way to make flag cards is to cut them out of a poster and paste them onto separate index cards. The only disadvantage to this method is that the resulting images will be so small that you will not be able to hold them up for the group to see as a whole. They will be appropriate for small group play but not larger group activities.

Method 2: If you want cards that will have more impact, make a photocopy of the black and white flags at the back of this book. Cut them up and copy again, enlarging 200 percent. Consult an almanac and use markers to color them. Paste onto index cards with countries' names below or on the backs. Laminate the cards and you're ready to go.

Method 3: If you'd like to cover your learning environment with large poster-sized flags of many nations, photocopy the desired flags from the back of this book and use an overhead projector to enlarge them to the desired size. Tack up your poster board so that the projected image falls directly on the poster board, and trace the design directly onto it. Consult your almanac and paint the flags with poster paint.

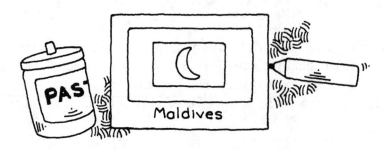

Maldives

Copyright © 1994, Good Apple

28

GA1486

Method **1.**

FLAGS

Cut from a poster...

and paste onto an index card.

Method **2.**

photo copy

enlarge

color and cut out

MARKERS

Sweden

Paste onto a card!

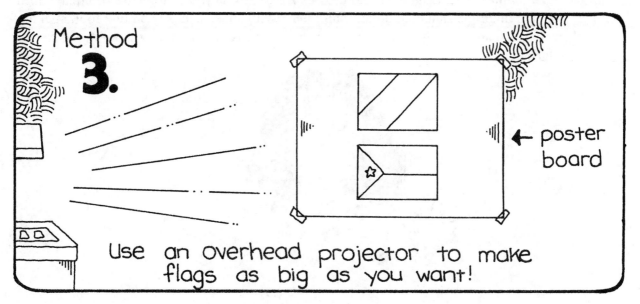

Method **3.**

← poster board

Use an overhead projector to make flags as big as you want!

Copyright © 1994, Good Apple

GA1486

Flags Together

The purpose of this activity is to familiarize the group with the basic colors, shapes, and forms of the flags; to observe the many ways in which flags are similar; and to point out their distinctive qualities. Displaying each flag with the name of the country to which it belongs has the added benefit of enabling the group to absorb the names of the countries of the world effortlessly.

Materials:

flag poster or flag cards
paper
pencil
chart (optional)

Begin by displaying your flags in a prominent place. Ask the group which color they think is found the most on the flags. Take a vote; then count the colors to see which one wins. Next ask how many flags have diagonal stripes, vertical stripes, stars, etc., and note the results.

Variations:

1. Make a chart which lists flags that have the following: star, moon, sun, cross, union jack, triangle, canton, circle, vertical stripes, horizontal stripes, diagonal stripes, animal, bird, flower, tree, fruit, shield, ship, water, landscape, people, unusual symbol, or writing. Count or list all the flags that belong to that group.

2. If you have separate flag cards that you have made or that go to another game, you can put them on the bulletin board under the headings listed above with their country names. You can do a few different headings each day.

3. Stand and Deliver: If you have separate flag cards, it's fun to give one to each person in the group and announce "diagonal stripes." Any person with a flag that has a diagonal stripe must stand up or come forward, etc. You can vary the commands each time, doing it so that players must think very quickly. For example, a person holding the card of Great Britain must stand up when red, white, blue, diagonals, and crosses are called. If you change the command each time, students might be standing, holding up their right hands, standing on one foot, sticking out their tongues, and putting their left hands behind their backs all at the same time. It can be pretty hilarious.

Copyright © 1994, Good Apple

GA1486

Fractured Flags

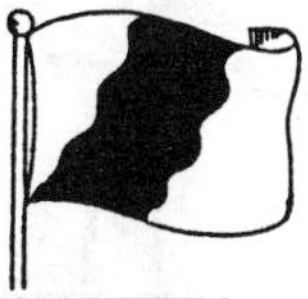

Materials:

flag poster or other ways of researching flags
paper
markers

Players:

two or more

Procedure:

Draw a picture of a familiar flag. Leave something out, or make it the wrong color or shape. Put the name of the country it belongs to underneath. Have the players identify the problem. (Note: Sometimes there can be more than one correct answer.)

Suggestion:

Fractured flags work well on student activity sheets. This idea can also be expressed as a multiple choice question (Figure 1). Children enjoy making up their own fractured flags and stumping their friends.

Multiple Choice:

Which of these looks the most like the flag of Japan?

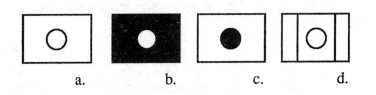

a.   b.   c.   d.

Figure 1

What's missing?

If this is the flag of India, what's missing?

Figure 2

What's wrong with this flag?

What's wrong with this Canadian flag?

Figure 3

Figure 3
Answer: maple leaf

Figure 2
Answer: wheel

Figure 1
Answer: c

Copyright © 1994, Good Apple

GA1486

Flag Matching

Based on the card game called Concentration.

Materials:
two sets of flag cards (see Flag Cards, page 28)
markers
scissors
Con-Tact™ paper

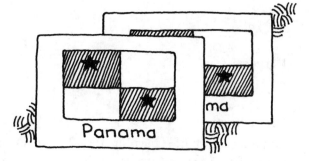

Players:
two

Preparation:
This activity requires two sets of flags. Start out with five pairs of flags that are the most familiar to the players. Many simple flags are provided in this book that you can reproduce. Color the flags (or have the group do it), cut them out, back each one with oaktag or cardboard for durability, and laminate.

Procedure:
Shuffle the flags and place them facedown on the table. Each player turns over two flags–first one flag, then another. If the flags match, the player goes again until he or she misses. Both cards are turned facedown again and the next player proceeds in the same way, moving any matches to his or her own winner's pile. Count the number of matches to determine the winner. The winner may then find the countries on a map that he or she "won."

Variation:
For more advanced play, use one set of flags without names to be matched with one set of name cards. This game is played in the same manner as above.

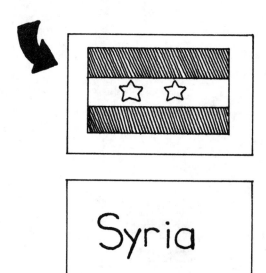

Copyright © 1994, Good Apple

GA1486

Flag Matching Concentration

Start with two of each flag.

Shuffle and place them facedown.

Turn over two cards one at a time. No match is scored. Turn cards over. Player 2 goes.

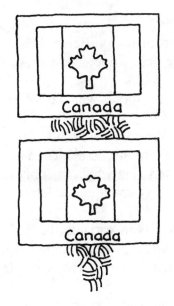

Two cards are turned over. A match is scored. The player removes these cards from the playing area and goes again.

Copyright © 1994, Good Apple

GA1486

Flag Roulette

Materials:

paper plate
plastic lid from a cottage cheese or yogurt container
hole punch
brass brad
colored markers
flags for reference (either book, poster, or cards)

Players:

two or more, or teams

Preparation:

Draw a large circle in the center of the paper plate and divide it into nine even sections. Color them red, white, blue, green, black, yellow, orange, brown, and light blue. Cut your cottage cheese container lid in the shape of an arrow and punch a hole in it large enough for the brad to hold it onto the center of the plate. The spinner should move freely.

Procedure:

Spin the plate. If the color comes up red, players must think of the name of a country whose flag has the color red in it. Whoever can do so successfully spins again until a flag can no longer be named containing that color or until he or she answers incorrectly. One point is scored for each correct answer.

Variations:

1. Instead of nine different colors, this time make a spinner with the following: shield, lion, flower, star, stripe, moon, dragon, bird, and sun.

2. Mix the symbols with the colors on the wheel.

3. Using the color wheel, the first player spins and tries to think of a flag that has only the color red. (There are none.) The next player spins and lands on the color white. If he or she can name any flag which has only the colors white and red on it, the player gets a point and goes again. Play continues as above.

4. Proceed as in variation three. Teams try to list as many flags as possible having the colors white and red, etc., within a time limit. You can't repeat flags that have already been named. No points are scored for same flags listed.

5. Mad Flags—If you want to have a lot of laughs, try combining this activity with Fractured Flags to create some really crazy flags.

Copyright © 1994, Good Apple

GA1486

Flag Roulette

Your Spinner

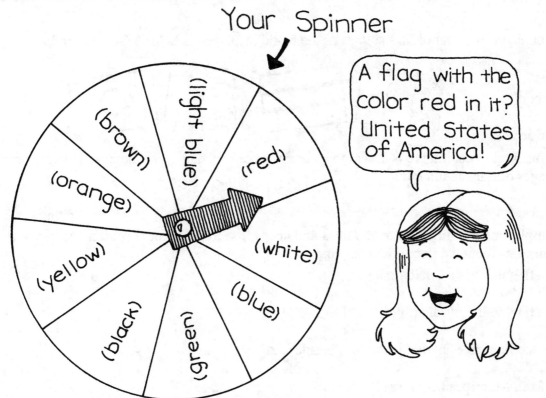

(light blue)
(brown)
(orange)
(yellow)
(black)
(green)
(blue)
(white)
(red)

A flag with the color red in it? United States of America!

(Photocopy and reduce these symbols. Glue them on a spinner. This will allow you to play variation 1.)

shield   lion   flower   star   stripe

moon   cross   bird   sun

Copyright © 1994, Good Apple

GA1486

Flagquisition

Materials:

none, but having a poster of all the flags of the world displayed is helpful (see Appendix)

Players:

two or more

Suggestion:

This game works best if there is access to a poster or book of flags. The almanac always contains a few pages of flags in full color.

Procedure:

The first player finds a flag he or she likes and keeps it secret. The next person has to ask a yes or no question about the flag. For example,

"Is it a flag that has a shield on it?"
"No."
"Is it a flag with vertical stripes?"
"Yes."
"Does the flag have anything else on it besides stripes?"
"No."
"Is it from a European country?"
"Yes."
"Does it have white in the middle stripe?"
"Yes."
"Is it France?"
"No."
"Is it Ireland?"
"Yes."

In this particular game it took seven guesses to name the flag. Points are scored for each guess made. The person or team with the least number of guesses wins.

Variations:

1. I Spy a Flag: The first player says, "I spy a flag with blue in it." The guessers try, one by one, to figure out which flag the person is looking at. Players may not change flags in mid game. Only one guess per person.

2. This can be played with place names. See Who Am I? on page 19.

Copyright © 1994, Good Apple

36

GA1486

Cultural Awareness Games

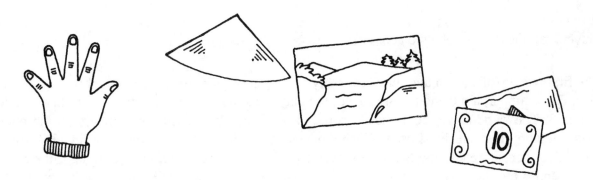

In this section you will find games played by children in other lands, foreign language games, and activities that will increase your appreciation and knowledge of other cultures.

Copyright © 1994, Good Apple

37

GA1486

Shut the Box

This is a popular game played by European children. A fancy version of it was sold in this country under the name of High Score. This game is a wonderful example of how a teacher using a thematic approach can incorporate math into the curriculum. Shut the Box originated in France and was commonly used by sailors in Normandy. It consisted of a box with numbered sections 1-9, hinged covers, and dice. For our purposes, however, the same game can be made with a piece of cardboard covered with Con-Tact™ paper and a few pennies or chips for markers.

Materials:
cardboard, bristol board, or oaktag
marker
Con-Tact™ paper
18 pennies or chips to mark the numbers
dice

1	2	3
4	5	6
7	8	9

Players:
one or more

Preparation:
Cut a piece of cardboard about 4" x 14" (10.16 x 35.56 cm). Divide it into nine equal sections. Write one of the numbers from 1 through 9 in each of the sections. Cover with Con-Tact™ paper.

Procedure:
Players roll the dice to see who goes first.

The first player rolls again and may cover any combination of numbers that equal the roll of the dice. For example, if a 6 and a 4 are rolled, the player can cover the 6 and the 4, the 10, or the 5, 3, and 2. The same player continues to roll and cover numbers until the numbers on the open spaces total 6; then one die is used. When a player can no longer use a number thrown to close a box, his or her turn ends, and the open spaces are totaled for the score. For example, if the numbers 3 and 4 are the only two numbers left and you roll an 8, no more moves can be made. At this point the remaining numbers are added up and 7 becomes your score. The next player tries to get a lower score. The object of the game is to cover as many numbers as possible until you are unable to do so on a given roll of the dice.

Variation:
Construction of the game can be simplified further if you don't have time to make a playing board. Number index cards from one to nine and turn them over to simulate closing the box covers, or simpler yet, using paper and pencil write the numbers from one to nine each time across the page, marking them out as you go.

Copyright © 1994, Good Apple

GA1486

Matreshka Nesting Dolls

Nesting dolls from Russia are a traditional folk toy representing the passing of one generation to the next. Each region of the Commonwealth of Independent States (formerly USSR) has its own traditional style of doll. The dolls are fun to play with, improve small muscle coordination, discrimination skills, and cultural awareness. See the Appendix for information on where to order them.

Copyright © 1994, Good Apple

GA1486

Finger Plays from Other Lands

Children derive great satisfaction from learning these simple action poems. Many of them are traditional rhymes that children in other lands learn from their mothers when they are very small. Kids love repeating them. It's the best way to learn numbers and other basic sounds and vocabulary effortlessly. You may use these with a flannel board or with finger movements. Here are a few in their original form and in translation. For more foreign language finger plays, consult your local library.

J'Irai dans le Bois:

Un, deux, trois, j'irai dans le bois, ("Ahn, Dur, Twa, Jheeray don le bwah")
Quatre, cinq, six, chercher les cerises, ("Katrah, sank, cease, share-shay lay sir-eese")
Sept, huit, neuf, dans mon panier neuf, ("Set, wheat, nuff, don moh panyay nuff")
Dix, onze, douze, elles seront toutes rouges. ("Dees, ohnz, dooz, el seron toot rouge")
Traditional

To the Woods Goes She

Four, five, six, cherries she picks;
Seven, eight, nine, in her basket fine;
Ten, eleven, twelve, she said,
All the cherries are red, red, red!
Traditional

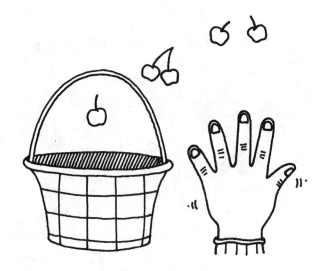

Conejito

Conejito que corre,
Que sube, que to alcanza,
Que te pilla y
Te tira la orejita
From Chile, Traditonal

Little Rabbit

Run, little rabbit; (Make hand run up arm with two fingers extended.)
Climb right up here. (Stop on the shoulder.)
He is so hungry (Move fingers around.)
He nibbles at my ear. (Pull on your ear.)

Copyright © 1994, Good Apple

GA1486

Lingo

As soon as a group of children learns the numbers of another language, you can play Lingo. This game is based on the old Italian game of Lotto dating from the 1500s, which has since evolved into the more familiar Bingo.

Materials:

poster board
chips or tokens to be used as markers
crayons or markers
Con-Tact™ paper

Players:

two or more

Preparation:

Divide an 8" x 10" (20.32 x 25.4 cm) piece of cardboard into eight squares and write a random number from 1-10 inside each square. Make one card for each player, with the numbers arranged differently on each card. Make sure all the numbers have been represented at least once somewhere in the set of cards. Then cut up more cardboard to make individual numbers from 1-10 for the caller. Laminate cards and numbers for durability.

Procedure:

Hand out a Lingo card to each player. Place the caller's cards facedown on the table. Appoint one person to be the caller. Numbers must be called in the foreign language. Players must use a token to cover the numbers called that appear on their cards. The first player to cover all the numbers on the card is the winner and becomes the caller for the next round.

Variation:

Use higher numbers or vocabulary words instead of the numbers 1 through 10.

Copyright © 1994, Good Apple

GA1486

Body Language

Here's a foreign language game that is guaranteed to have everyone in stitches!

Materials:

stickers

markers or a computer

Players:

two or more, but the more the merrier

Preparation:

Write the names for the parts of the body on stickers in the language you are learning and have a set of these for each player.

Procedure:

Players pair off and take turns sticking the labels on the appropriate body parts of their partners. Switch and give the other person a turn. Care should be taken not to injure property, clothing, or persons.

Copyright © 1994, Good Apple

GA1486

Hats of Many Lands

Materials:

authentic hats from other lands
recordings of ethnic music from other lands
record player or tape machine

Players:

five or more

Hats to Consider:

Middle Eastern fez or turban, Chinese coolie hat, Spanish mantilla, Spanish bullfighter's hat, French beret, Mexican sombrero, Portuguese fisherman's cap, Russian shapka fur hat, Australian cowboy hat, British derby, Irish cap, Dutch woman's linen cap, Moroccan scull cap, Peruvian bowler hat, Japanese straw hat, Jewish yarmulke, Indian Ghandi cap, etc.

Procedure:

Place the hat on the head of one of the players. Turn the music on and let it play for a minute or two. While this is happening, players carefully pass the hat from one head to the next. When the music stops, the person caught with the hat leads the others in a dance once around in a circle.

Variations:

Collage:

Gather pictures of hats from around the world and talk about what lands they come from. Paste pictures of hats onto appropriate continent maps. Talk about why people wear them and what meanings they have.

Hatbox:

Collect or make hats of other lands. Keep them in a box and use them for dress-up in your learning environment. Cut out pictures of native peoples wearing similar hats and provide a mirror.

Relay Race:

Collect hats and/or native costumes in two boxes, one for each team. The first player must run up to the box, dress in a native costume consisting of a specified number of garments (or just a hat if that is all you have) as quickly as possible. Then the player must run back and help dress the next runner. As soon as the next runner has donned the costume, he or she must run to the box, undress, replace the costume in the box, run back, and tag the next runner. Play proceeds in this manner. The first team finished wins.

Copyright © 1994, Good Apple

GA1486

Collections

Collecting and displaying things from other lands is a great way to engender a natural interest in the world beyond our borders. Here are some suggestions for the things you might collect as well as activities to enrich your learning environment:

postcards
hats
real flags or flag reproductions
artifacts
authentic crafts
dolls wearing traditional costumes
souvenirs
toys or games
coins, foreign currency
foreign postage stamps
newspapers and magazines written in other languages
picture books in other languages
clothing
road maps
food or recipes

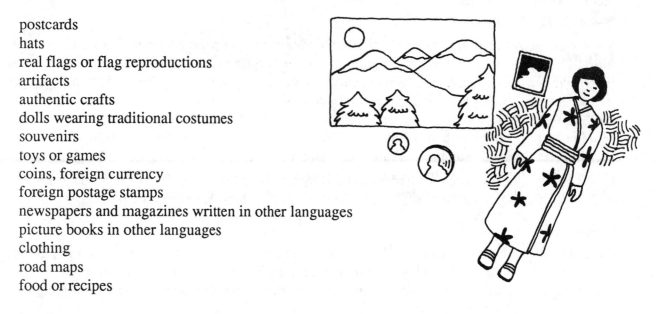

Postcards:

Put postcards on your bulletin board around a large map of the world with a bright piece of yarn or string leading to the location on the map of the place they depict.

Picture Books:

Many libraries have picture books in other languages. Often it is possible to find the same book in English. Display the books together if you can, so that children can compare the two and practice saying the foreign words. If you have native speakers in your class, ask them to read the story out loud. Then have someone read the English.

Fashion Show:

Have children model some of the costumes you've collected with someone reading a description of the clothing worn and its function, symbolism, etc. Music may be added.

Food:

Ask each person in the group to prepare an ethnic dish to share. Display the recipe along with the food.

Road Maps:

Plan a trip by car in a foreign land. Where will you stay? What will you see?

Copyright © 1994, Good Apple

GA1486

Collections

Show and Tell:

Ask kids to bring in specific things related to your unit (for example, photos from foreign lands, artifacts, clothing, postcards, stamps, foreign currency, etc.).

Travel Talk:

Sit in a circle. Ask children to share travel experiences they or people in their families have had. Introduce this activity and invite children to bring in family photos, postcards, or artifacts from those places they visited. See if children can locate on a map where they went. How did they get there? How long did it take? What was the weather like? What was different about the place they visited? Where did they stay? Did they see any mountains? Cross any big rivers?

Guests:

If you know people who have traveled to faraway places, ask them to visit your group and show slides, talk about their travels, and pass around things they may have acquired on their trips.

Copyright © 1994, Good Apple

GA1486

World Bank

Materials:

foreign currency, or pictures of foreign paper money
U.S. or Canadian play money
almanac or other source for consulting current exchange rates
paper
scissors
copy machine

Players:

two or more

Preparation:

Make photocopies of the foreign currency on the next page. Also get play money of American or Canadian currency. Post a list of the foreign exchange rates. Choose one player to be the banker. Hand out foreign currency to be exchanged.

Procedure:

Players bring their foreign currency to the "bank" and exchange it for copies of U.S. or Canadian money or vice versa.

Note:

Included on page 47 are denominations that will require both multiplication and division: 2 Philipino Pisos, 5,000,000 Nicaraguan Cordobas, 5 English Pounds, 10 Kenyan Shillings, 100 Ukranian Rubles, and One Guatemalan Quetzal.

Variations:

If the math is too challenging for your group, try rounding out the exchange rate, choosing countries whose exchange rates are easiest to deal with, or making up a pretend rate of exchange based upon the skill level of the group.

Copyright © 1994, Good Apple

GA1486

Copyright © 1994, Good Apple

GA1486

Creative Dramatics

Someone once said, "Travel is the best teacher." Well, creative dramatics is the next best thing to traveling. Here are a few examples of how you can use imagination to take you anywhere in the world and beyond.

Blast Off:

Take an imaginary trip from home to the outer reaches of the universe. This exercise teaches children to visualize the spatial relationships between city, state, country, planet, and finally solar system. The more detail you go into describing the things you see from above, the better. You can talk about everything from the Alps to the Gobi desert and present vocabulary that will be absorbed effortlessly.

Magic Carpet Ride:

Take an imaginary trip to a faraway land. "We're going on a magic carpet ride! Everyone aboard!" Be sure to describe how the place looks (are there mountains, cities, etc.), its climate, whether there is snow, or perhaps desert. Picture what it's like to walk around there. Choose some of the sights and describe them (for example, the Great Wall of China, the Eiffel Tower, the Great Pyramids), how the people are dressed, what they're doing, what you're eating for supper, etc. After your journey, try to get a postcard or some photos from *National Geographic, Geo,* or some other magazine showing the place you visited on your magic carpet ride and place it next to your world map with a piece of yarn pointing to where it is found on the map.

A Gift for the Earth:

Take an imaginary walk in a beautiful place with your group. Experience each of your senses as you describe this place to the group. If you aren't capable of "making it up as you go along," write out a few notes ahead of time so that you "climb a beautiful snow-covered mountain" and then descend into a lush green valley or whatever picture you wish to paint. Then in this peaceful place have everyone leave a gift for the earth. Ask participants to share with the group what each left and why, or have participants draw the gift.

Copyright © 1994, Good Apple

GA1486

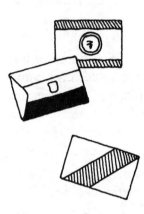

Appendix

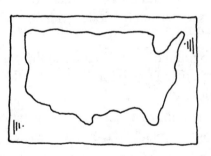

In this section you will find a listing of helpful teaching materials, books, catalogs, outline maps and flags and where to find them.

Every effort has been made, at the time of publication, to insure the accuracy of the information and maps included in this book. We cannot guarantee, however, that the agencies and organizations we have mentioned will continue to operate or to maintain these current locations indefinitely.

Copyright © 1994, Good Apple

GA1486

Appendix

Teaching Materials:

Dymaxion World Puzzle Map. Invented by Buckminster Fuller. This map has no up and down or should be. Puzzle consists of 20 wooden triangles. Available from Michael Olaf (see catalog listing).

Faces: The Magazine About People. Published monthly except in June, July, and August. Cobblestone Publishing, Inc., 7 School Street, Peterboro, NH 03458, (603) 924-7902. Parent's Choice Magazine Award Winner.

National Flags of the World Wall Chart. Available from the Flag Research Center, Winchester, MA 01890. This chart is updated regularly and can be cut up and used to make many other useful learning materials.

The Peter Projection Map. Shows the earth from the equator with the real size and area of the land masses. Also includes small reproductions of the "normal" map along the bottom for comparison. This map is a real eye-opener. (Also see *A New View of the World* in the book section for ideas on how to use this map.)

Commercial Games:

Famous Cities Quartet Game. From Piatnik Company of Austria. A card game involving cities of the world. Full-color cards depicting places of interest in well-known international cities.

Flags. From RDN Games, Division of Publibec Limited, Sorel (Quebec), Canada J3R 4R4. Contains world gameboard; 255 cards of capitals, flags, currency and languages; and flag guess card. In French and English.

Friends Around the World. A game of world peace for two to four players ages five and up. Cooperative game including sixteen international friends with biographical sketches. Available from Aristoplay (see catalog listing).

Global Pursuit. National Geographic's contribution to the game market. This game features various skill levels, as well as a terrific Dymaxion World Puzzle Map which players put together as they answer geography questions correctly.

Journey Through Europe. Familiarizes children with names of major cities of Europe; the important sights; and travelling by boat, plane or over land.

Mile Bornes. By Parker Brothers. An exciting bilingual card game (French/English) which involves some simple math skills.

Our Town. Ages 4 to 8, two to four players. Personalized by wipe-off names on houses and stores. Teaches awareness of local geography.

Take Off! A recipient of the Parent's Choice Award. Players start off in Hawaii. The first to complete an around-the-world flight wins. Teaches countries, cities, flags, etc.

Where in the World. Comes with map boards of major land areas, cards depicting flags, and vital statistics of each country, etc. Some of the flags, statistics, and maps are now out-of-date.

Catalogs:

Animal Town, P.O. Box 485, Healdsburg, CA 95448, (800) 445-8642. A catalog of multicultural games (many are cooperative), books, toys, and crafts.

Aristoplay, P.O. Box 7529, Ann Arbor, MI 48107, (800) 634-7738. Good source for educational games.

Copyright © 1994, Good Apple

GA1486

The Daily Planet/Russian Dressing, P.O. Box 1313, New York, NY 10013, (212) 807-7200. Great source for matreshka dolls and other Russian artifacts.

Elderly Instruments, 1100 N. Washington, P.O. Box 14210, Lansing, MI 48901, (517) 372-7890. Carries an amazing collection of recordings from all over the world as well as instruments.

Everyone's Kids Books, 71 Elliott St., Brattleboro, VT 05301. Best collection of multiracial, cultural books I've seen. Catalog contains lengthy descriptions of books and appropriate ages.

Michael Olaf, P.O. Box 1162, Arcata, CA 95521. Montessori and other interesting learning materials for pre-k through 6.

North South Books, Inc., 1133 Broadway, Suite 1016, New York, NY 10010, (800) 282-8257. Publishes a series of picture books in English, German, and French.

Books for Parents and Teachers:

America in Fourteen Ninety-Two: The World of the Indian Peoples Before the Arrival of Columbus edited by Alvin Josephy (Knopf, 1992). Pre-Columbian culture, arts, languages, political and social life.

Art from Many Hands by Jo Miles Schuman. (Davis, 1981). Multicultural art projects that kids can make. Easy-to-follow directions, and the final products look great!

The Book of Where; Or How to Be Naturally Geographic by Neill Bell. (Little Brown, 1982).

A Children's Almanac of Words at Play by Willard R. Espy. (Clarkson N. Potter, Inc., 1982). Look under "Jumbled Geography," and "In the Foreign Fashion" in the index for a number of interesting geography games.

Crafts of Many Cultures by Aurelia Gomez. (Scholastic, 1992).

Creative Drama in the Classroom by Nellie McCaslin. (Longman, 1984).

Don't Know Much About Geography by Kenneth C. Davis. (William and Morrow, 1992). Explores such interesting questions as Who killed the Dead Sea? What's so bad about the Badlands? as well as a list of names and nicknames of the fifty American states.

Flags Through the Ages and Across the World by Dr. Whitney Smith. (McGraw-Hill, 1975). The best book on flags available. As with all geographic material these days a lot of the flags are out-of-date, but the historical and descriptive information more than make up for it. This book is out of print so you will have to check your local library.

Games of the World by Frederick D. Grunfeld. (Swiss Committee for UNICEF, 1975). A wonderful collection of indoor and outdoor games, how to make them, and how to play them.

Guide to the Flags of the World by Mauro Talocci. (Quill, 1982). No longer up-to-date but provides a paperback reference book on flags, their symbolism, and history.

I Hate Charades by Phil Wiswell. (Sterling Publishing Co., 1981). Contains many games that can be transformed into geography games as well as Borderlines which involves picking a state or country and trying to guess which states or countries border it.

Keepers of the Animals: Native American Stories and Wildlife Activities for Children by Michael Caduto and Joseph Bruchac. (Fulcrum, 1991).

Kwanzaa: An African-American Celebration of Culture and Cooking by Eric V. Copage. (Morrow, 1991). Recipes from Africa and all over the Americas as well as stories to illustrate the seven principles of Kwanzaa, a relatively new holiday created to focus on African values and culture.

Copyright © 1994, Good Apple

GA1486

Appendix

The Mapmakers: The Story of the Great Pioneers in Cartography–From Antiquity to the Space Age by John Noble Wilford. (Knopf, 1981).

Names of the Land: A Historical Account of Place Naming in the United States by George R. Stewart. (Houghton Mifflin, 1958).

Names on the Globe by George R. Stewart. (Oxford, 1975). Explains the origins of many place names around the world.

New View of the World: A Handbook to the World Map by Ward Kaiser. History of world maps, comparisons with other maps, and ideas for using the Peter Projection Map.

The People Atlas by Phillip Steele. (Oxford University Press, 1991). Based on people rather than boundaries. A valuable reference to the great diversity of human life including food, clothing, and traditions.

Place Names of the World by Adrian Room. (Angus and Robertson, 1987).

Rhymes for Fingers and Flannel Boards by Louise Binder Scott and J.J. Thompson. (McGraw-Hill, 1960). Contains an entire section devoted to finger plays from other lands.

Roots and Wings Affirming Culture in Early Childhood Programs by Stacey York. (Toys 'n Things Press, 1991).

State of the Earth Atlas by Joni Seager. How each nation impacts the world. Compares acid rain levels, tourism, forestation, air quality, resource use, etc.

Steven Caney's Toy Book. (Workman Publishing Co., 1972). This book contains an excellent method for making durable puzzles by cutting up old road maps, etc., and dipping the pieces in a glue/water mixture. Pieces dry clear and you can see the lines underneath.

Teaching Games for Fun by Linda Polon and Wendy Pollitt. (T.S. Denison & Co., Inc., 1976). This book contains a few geography games but also has some ideas for incorporating geography into games that teach other skills. This can be helpful for teachers using a thematic approach.

Toposaurus: A Humorous Treasury of Toponyms (familiar words and phrases derived from place names) by John D. Jacobson. (John Wiley & Sons, 1990).

Where on Earth: A Refreshing View of Geography by Donnat V. Grillet. (Prentice Hall, 1991).

The World Is Burning: Murder in the Rain Forest by Alex Shoumatoff. (Little Brown, 1990).

The World's Best Travel Games by Sheila Anne Barry. (Sterling Publishing Co., 1987). A big help if you're planning a trip with your family or school!

Young Peacemakers Project Book by Kathleen Fry-Miller and Judith Myers-Walls. (Brethren Press, 1988). Devotes an entire chapter to projects for "People All over the World."

Books for Children:

Annie . . . Anya: A Month in Moscow by Irene Trivas. (Orchard, 1992).

Anno's U.S.A. by Mitsumasa Anno. (Putnam/Philomel, 1983). Wordless.

Bread, Bread, Bread by Ann Morris. (Lothrop, Lee, Shepard, 1989). Illustrated with photographic examples from all over the world and maps to locate each place.

Children of the Yukon by Ted Harrison. (Tundra Books, 1977). Describes the life of the people of Northern Canada.

Chin Chiang and the Dragon's Dance by Ian Wallace. (Atheneum, 1984). Asian-American story.

Copyright © 1994, Good Apple

Appendix

Clambake: A Wamkpanoag Tradition by Russell Peters. (Lerner, 1992). Mashpee Wampanoag tribe on Cape Cod. Illustrated with photographs.

Count on Your Fingers African Style by Claudia Zaslavsky. (Crowell, 1980).

The Cows Are Going to Paris by David Kirby and Allen Woodman. (Caroline House, 1991).

Day of Ahmed's Secret by Florence Parry Heide. (Lothrop, Lee, and Shepard, 1990). Shows daily life in Cairo, Egypt.

Down Under by Jan Reynolds from the Vanishing Cultures Series. (Harcourt, Brace, Jovanovich, 1992). Illustrated with photographs. Describes the Tiwi people, an aboriginal tribe off northern coast of Australia.

The Facts on File Children's Atlas by David and Jill Wright. (Facts on File, 1989).

Far North by Jan Reynolds from the Vanishing Cultures Series. (Harcourt, Brace, Jovanovich, 1992). Illustrated with photographs. Story of Sami family from the Lapland.

Flags of the United Nations Sticker Book by Jan and Frank Asch and Sue Leland. (Scholastic, 1990). Reusable flag stickers, activities, maps, and vital statistics.

Galimoto by Karen Lynn Williams. (Lothrop, Lee, and Shepard, 1990). Realistic portrait of contemporary village life in Malawi, Africa.

The Geography Coloring Book by Wynn Kapit. (Harper/Collins, 1991).

Geography Puzzles by Peggy Adler. (Franklin Watts, 1979). This book contains some terrific geography rebuses (picture puzzles).

The Giraffe That Walked to Paris by Nancy Milton. (Crown, 1992).

Hats, Hats, Hats, by Ann Morris. (Lothrop, Lee, and Shepard, 1989).

Himalaya by Jan Reynolds from the Vanishing Cultures Series. (Harcourt, Brace, Jovanovich, 1991). Illustrated with photographs. Story of a young Sherpa girl and her family.

Houses and Homes by Ann Morris. (Morrow, 1992). Illustrated with photographic examples from all over the world and maps to locate each place.

Kwanzaa by A.P. Porter. (Carolrhoda Books, 1991). History and rituals of this African-American holiday.

Let's Go Traveling by Robin Rector Krupp. (Morrow, 1992).

Magic Carpet by Pat Brisson. (Bradbury, 1991).

The Magic School Bus Lost in the Solar System by Joanna Cole. (Scholastic, 1990).

The Moon Lady by Amy Tan. (Macmillan, 1992). Chinese story by the author of *The Joy Luck Club*.

My Place in Space by Robin and Sally Hirst. (Orchard Books, 1988).

My Uncle Nikos by Judy Delton. (Crowell, 1983).

Nine O'Clock Lullaby by Marilyn Singer. (Harper/Collins, 1991). Shows what's happening at various locations around the world when it's bedtime in Brooklyn.

People by Peter Spier. (Doubleday, 1980).

The Pop-Up Atlas of the World by Theodore Rowland-Entwistle. Illustrated by Phil Jacobs and Mike Peterkin. (Simon & Schuster, 1988).

Sahara by Jan Reynolds from the Vanishing Cultures Series. (Harcourt, Brace, Jovanovich, 1991). Illustrated with photographs. Story of the Tuareg, a nomadic people.

Copyright © 1994, Good Apple

GA1486

Sami and the Time of the Troubles by Florence Parry Heide and Judith Heide Gilliland. (Clarion Books, 1992). A child's eye view of Beirut and its problems.

Shabanu, Daughter of the Wind by Suzanne Fisher Staples. (Knopf/Random House, 1989). Glimpse into traditional Moslem culture of Pakistan as seen through the eyes of a young girl.

The Sign in Mendel's Window by Mildred Phillips. (Macmillan, 1985). Story set in Kosnov, Russia.

Silent Lotus by Jeanne M. Lee. (Farrar, Strauss, and Giroux, 1991). Story takes place in a rural village in ancient Kampuchea.

Somewhere in Africa by Ingrid Mennen and Niki Daly. (Dutton, 1992).

Step into China by Neil Johnson. (Messner, 1988). Basic introduction to China illustrated with photographs of children in everyday activities.

Take One Compass by Melvin Berger. (Scholastic, 1990). This book comes with a compass and contains some interesting geography games and activities which will increase awareness of directions, maps, charting the movements of the sun and moon throughout the day.

This Is My House by Arthur Dorros. (Scholastic, 1992). Children from twenty different countries describe their homes.

Tools by Ann Morris. (Morrow, 1992). Illustrated with photographic examples from all over the world and maps to locate each place.

You Can Write Chinese by Kurt Wiese. (Viking 1945).

Folktales:

Arctic Memories by Normee Ekoomiak. (Holt, 1990). Art and text describe both traditional and current ways of life of people of the far North.

Ayu and the Perfect Moon by David Cox. (The Bodley Head, 1984). Bali.

The Banza by Diane Wolkstein. (Dial, 1981). Haiti.

The Bird Who Cleans the World and Other Mayan Fables by Victor Montejo. (Curbstone, 1991).

Borreguita and the Coyote by Verna Aardema. (Random House, 1991). Humorous tale from Aylta, Mexico.

Bringing the Rain to Kapiti Plain by Verna Aardema. (Scholastic, 1989). African tale.

The Cat Who Loved to Sing by Nonny Hogrogian. (Alfred A. Knopf/Borzoi Books, 1988). Armenian folktale.

Clever Tom and the Leprechaun: An Old Irish Story by Linda Shute. (Lothrop, Lee, and Shepard Books, 1988).

The Crystal Flower and the Sun by Farida Fardjam. (Persia).

Dragon Kite of the Autumn Moon by Valerie Reddix. (Lothrop, Lee, and Shepard, 1992). Taiwanese story.

Elinda Who Danced in the Sky: An Estonian Folktale adapted by Lynn Moroney. (Children's Book Press, 1990).

The Emperor and the Kite by Jane Yolen. (Philomel Books, 1988). Chinese folktale.

The Enchanted Umbrella by Odette Meyers. (Harcourt, Brace, Jovanovich/Gulliver Books, 1988). French folktale.

Finn Mac Cool and the Small Men of Deed by Pat O'Shea. (Holiday House, 1987). Irish.

Copyright © 1994, Good Apple

GA1486

The Five Chinese Brothers by Claire Huchet Bishop and Kurt Wiese. (Coward McCann, 1938, 1989). This book has been translated into many different languages. Check your local library for foreign language editions.

The Ghost and the Lone Warrior by C.J. Taylor. (Tundra Books, 1991). Arapaho legend.

Goat in the Rug by Charles L. Blood and Martin Link. (Four Winds Press, 1980). How a Navajo rug is woven in fable form.

The Hallowed Horse by Demi. (Dodd, Mead, 1987). Indian folktale.

The Hedgehog Boy: A Latvian Folktale by Jane Langton. (Harper and Row, 1985).

How Raven Freed the Moon by Anne Cameron. (Harbour Publications, 1985).

How the Loon Lost Her Voice by Anne Cameron. (Harbour Publications, 1985).

How Two-Feather Was Saved from Loneliness by C.J. Taylor. (Tundra Books, 1990). Abenaki legend of the beginning of time.

Judge Rabbit & the Tree Spirit by Linda Mao Wall. (Children's Book Press, 1991). Folktale from Cambodia.

Lazy Boy by Anne Cameron. (Harbour Publications, 1988).

The Legend of El Dorado by Beatriz Vidal. (Knopf, 1991). Latin American legend of Lake Titicaca.

Little Water and the Gift of the Animals by C.J. Taylor. (Tundra Books, 1992). Canadian Mohawk tale.

Louhi, Witch of North Far by Toni de Gerez. (Viking Kestrel, 1986). Finnish folktale.

The Mysterious Giant of Barletta by Tomie de Paola. (Harcourt, Brace, Jovanovich, 1984). Italy.

Orca's Song by Anne Cameron. (Harbour Publications, 1987).

Owl in the Cedar Tree by Natachee Scott Momaday. (Univ. of Nebraska Press, 1992). Navaho story.

Patronella by Betty Waterton. (Vanguard, 1981).

The People Who Hugged the Trees by Deborah Lee Rose. (Roberts Rinehart, 1990) A Legend of Rajasthan, India.

Pueblo Storyteller by Diane Hoyt-Goldsmith. (Holiday House, 1991). Illustrated with full-color photographs.

Raven Returns the Water by Anne Cameron. (Harbour Publications, 1987).

Return of the Sun by Joseph Bruchac. (Crossing Press, 1989). Tales of native people of Northeast woodlands.

The Riddle of the Drum: A Tale from Tizapan, Mexico, by Verna Aardema. (Four Winds Press, 1978).

Sedna, an Eskimo Myth by Beverly Brodsky McDermott.

Sooshewan, Child of the Beothuk by Donald Gale. Story from Newfoundland.

Spider Woman by Anne Cameron. (Harbour Publications, 1988).

The Star Maiden by Barbara Juster Esbensen. (Little Brown, 1988). Adapted from story written by Chief of Ojibway nation in 1850.

Suho and the White Horse: A Legend of Mongolia by Yuzo Otsuka.

Toad Is the Uncle of Heaven: A Vietnamese Folk Tale. by Jeanne M. Lee. (Holt, Rinehart and Winston, 1985). Vietnamese tale.

Copyright © 1994, Good Apple

GA1486

Appendix

The Tongue-Cut Sparrow by Momoko Ishii. (Dutton/Lodestar Books, 1987). Japanese folktale.

Tonweya and the Eagles and Other Lakota Tales by Rosebud Yellow Robe. Traditional stories of the Lakota people.

The Turtle and the Island by Barbara Ker Wilson. (Lippincott, 1990). Tale from Papua, New Guinea.

The Village of Round and Square Houses by Ann Grifalconi. (Little, Brown, 1986). From *The Cameroons*. (Caldecott honor book and notable trade book in the field of social studies.).

Who's in Rabbit's House by Verna Aardema. (Dial, 1977). Masai (African) folktale.

Why Mosquitos Buzz in People's Ears by Verna Aardema. (Scholastic, 1975). West Africa.

Bilingual Books:

Desert Mermaid by Alberto Bianco. (Children's Book Press, 1992). Spanish/English set in Sonora Desert.

Here Comes the Cat by Frank Asch and Vladimir Vagin. (Scholastic, 1989). A wonderful story in English and Russian about mice and a cat whose relationship is surprising.

My Mother the Mail Carrier/Mi Mama La Cartera by Inez Maury. (Feminist Press).

The Paperbag Princess by Rubert Munsch. (Annick Press, 1991). *La Princesa Vestida con Una Bolsa De Papel* (Firefly Books, 1991). Spanish edition.

Song of the Chirimia/La Musica De La Chirimia by Jane Volkmer. (Lerner, 1992). Guatemalan folktale. Illustrations based on ancient Mayan stone carvings. Bilingual.

The Woman Who Outshone the Sun by Aljejandro Cruz Martinez. Legend of the Zapotec Indians of Mexico. (Children's Book Press, 1991). Spanish/English.

Hope you've found this book fun and rewarding!

Copyright © 1994, Good Apple

GA1486

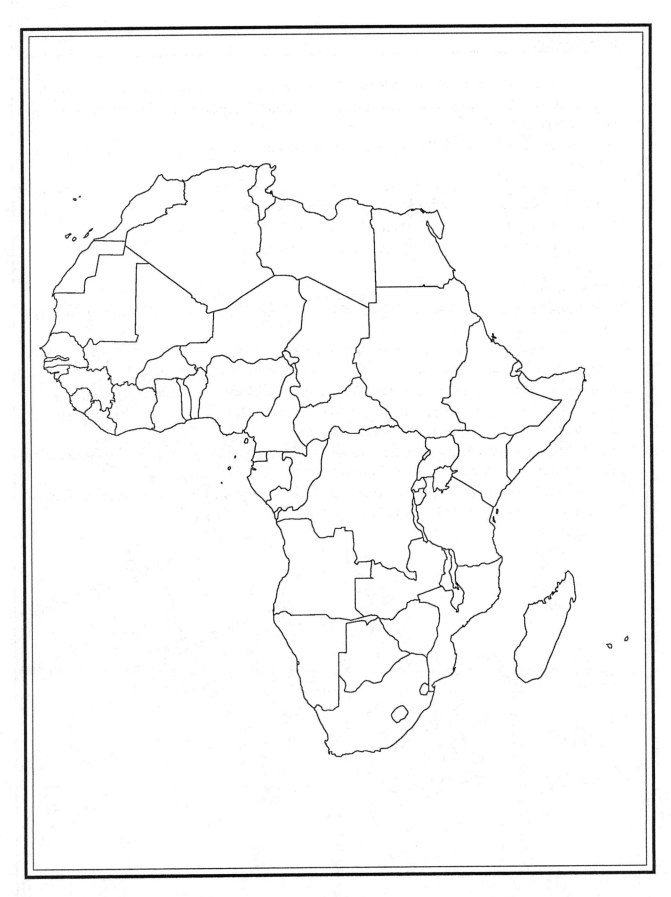

Africa

Copyright © 1994, Good Apple

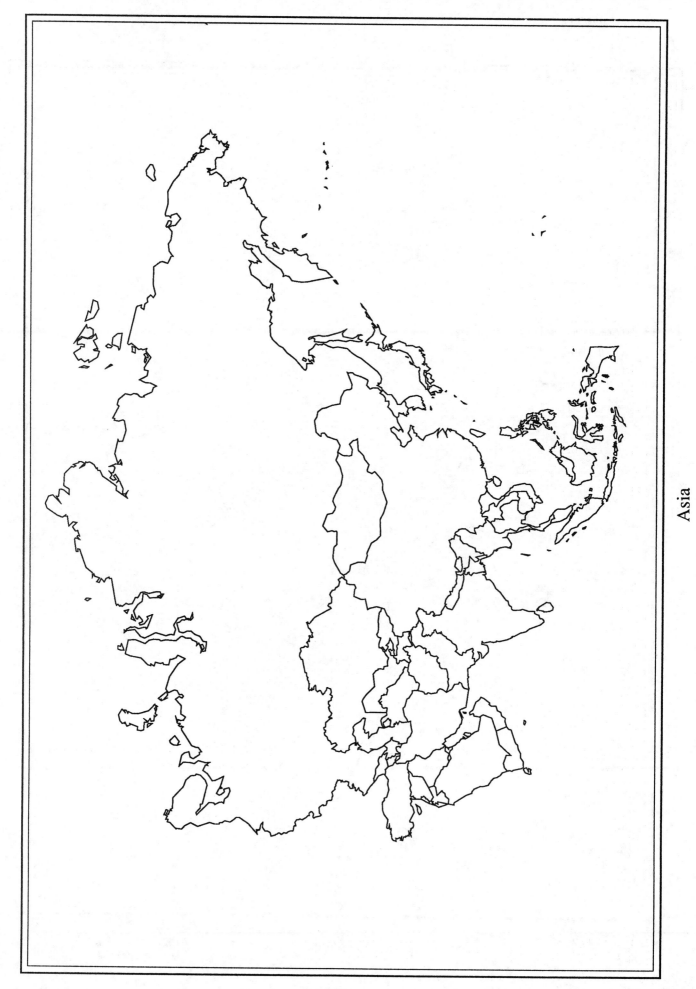

Asia

Copyright © 1994, Good Apple

58

GA1486

Canada

Copyright © 1994, Good Apple

GA1486

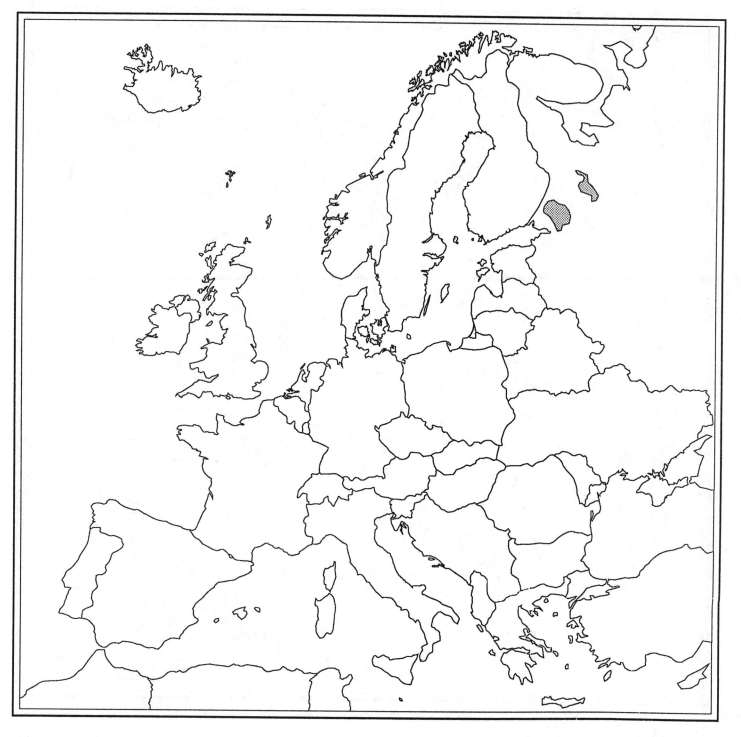

Europe

Copyright © 1994, Good Apple

60

GA1486

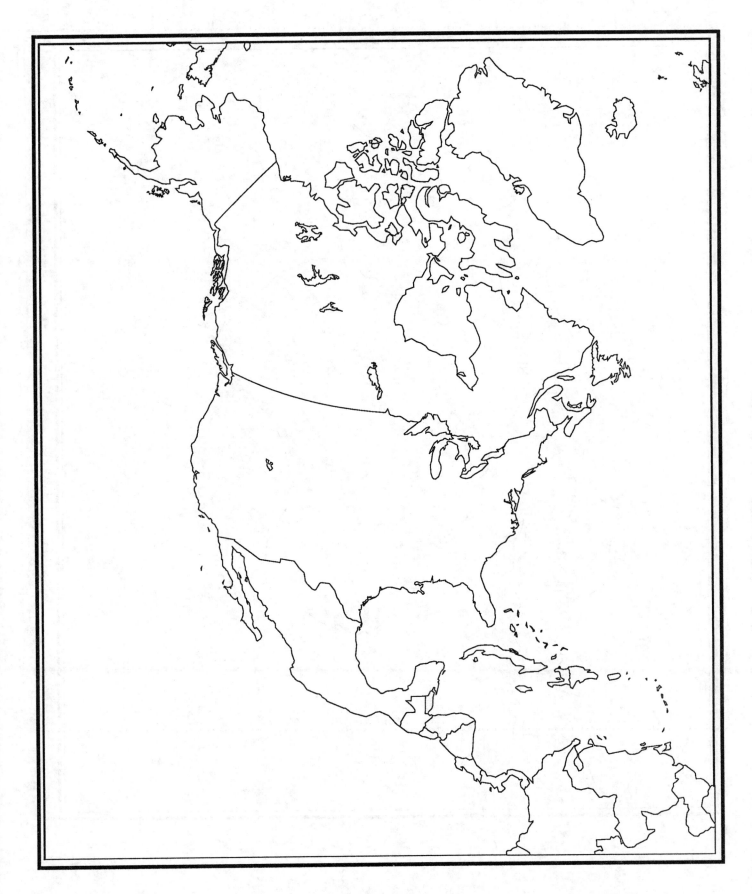

North and Central America

Copyright © 1994, Good Apple

61

GA1486

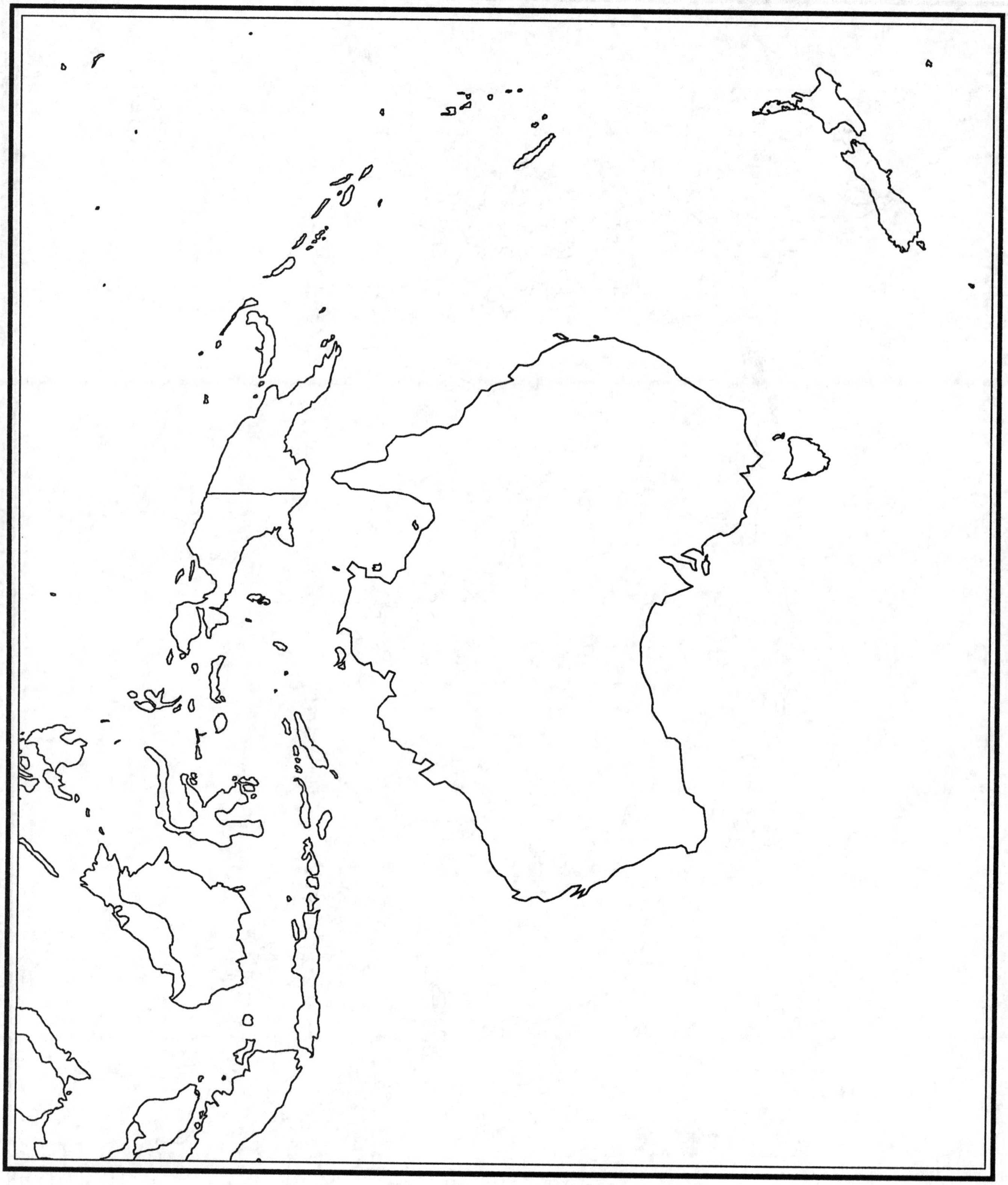

Copyright © 1994, Good Apple

Oceania

GA1486

South America

Copyright © 1994, Good Apple

63

GA1486

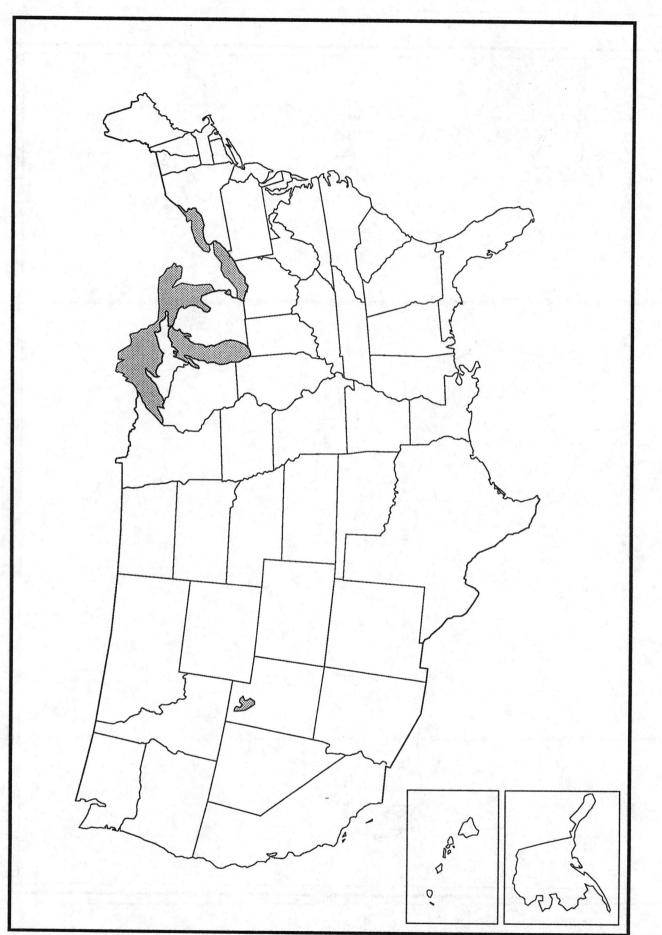

United States

Copyright © 1994, Good Apple

64

GA1486

Albania

Algeria

Armenia, Austria, Bulgaria, Estonia,
Gabon, Germany, Hungary, Netherlands
Russia, Sierra Leone, Yemen

Argentina

Bahrain

Australia

Bangladesh

Belize

Copyright © 1994, Good Apple

65

GA1486

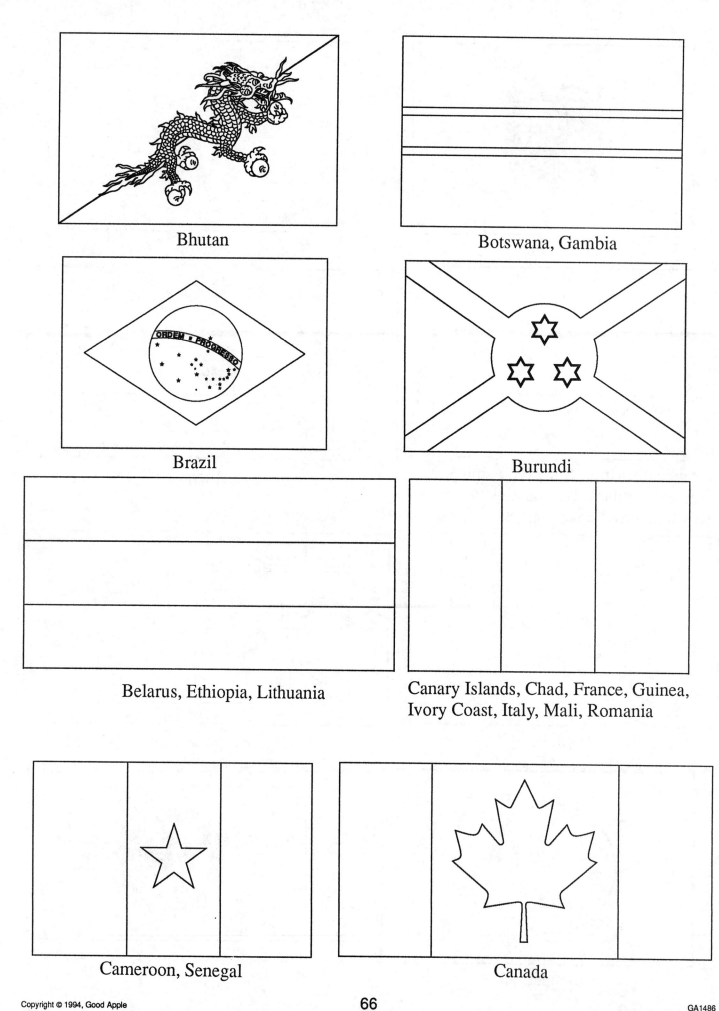

Bhutan

Botswana, Gambia

Brazil

Burundi

Belarus, Ethiopia, Lithuania

Canary Islands, Chad, France, Guinea,
Ivory Coast, Italy, Mali, Romania

Cameroon, Senegal

Canada

Copyright © 1994, Good Apple

66

GA1486

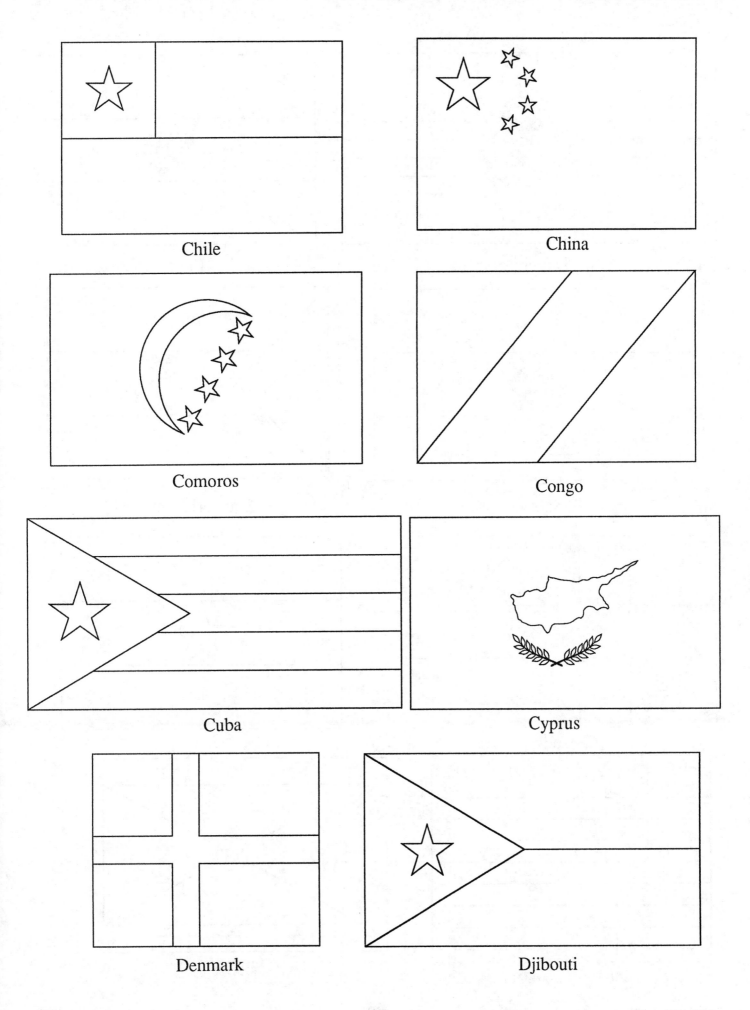

Chile

China

Comoros

Congo

Cuba

Cyprus

Denmark

Djibouti

Copyright © 1994, Good Apple

GA1486

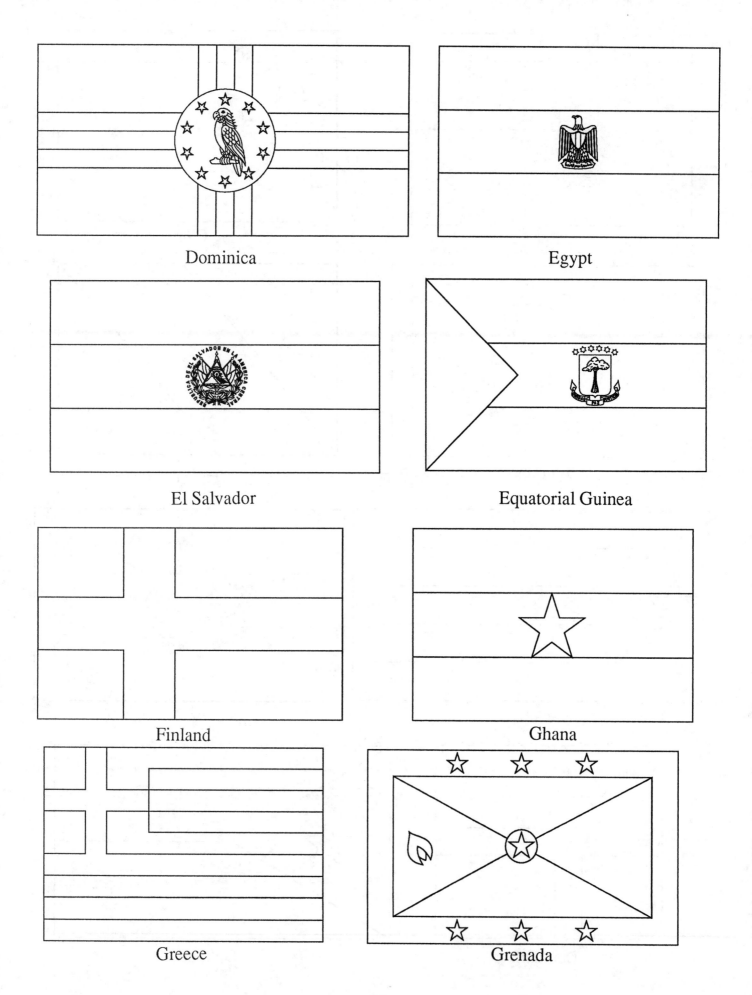

Dominica

Egypt

El Salvador

Equatorial Guinea

Finland

Ghana

Greece

Grenada

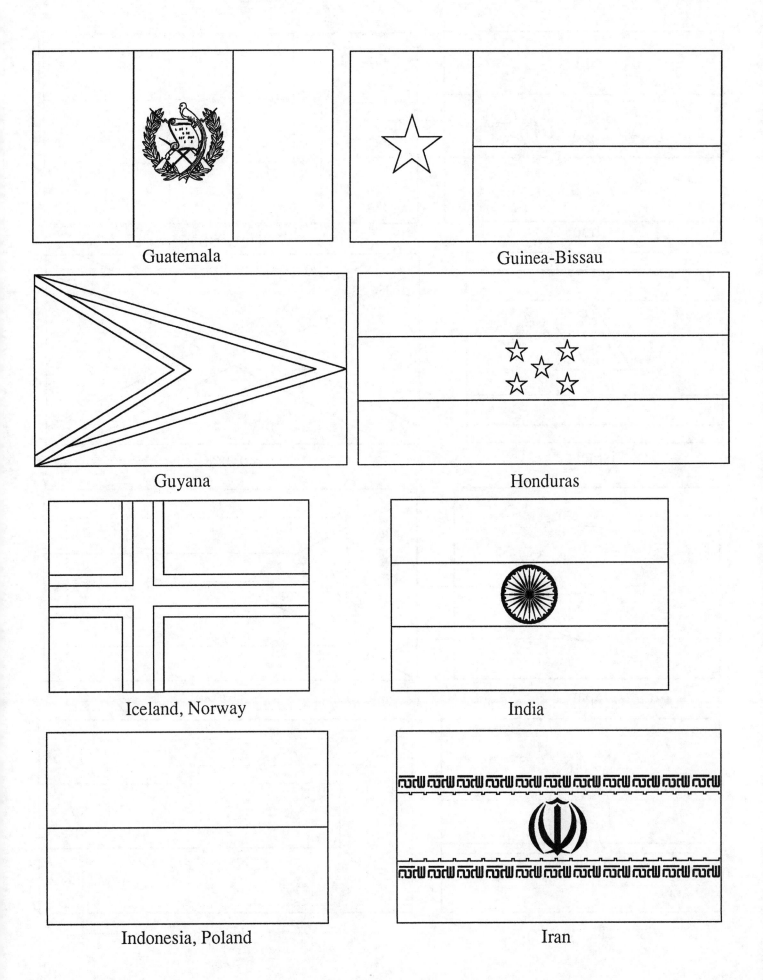

Guatemala

Guinea-Bissau

Guyana

Honduras

Iceland, Norway

India

Indonesia, Poland

Iran

Copyright © 1994, Good Apple

GA1486

Iraq

Ireland, Nigeria

Israel

Jamaica

Japan

Jordan

Kenya

Kuwait

Copyright © 1994, Good Apple

Laos

Lebanon

Lesotho

Liberia

Libya

Maldives

Malaysia

Mexico

Morocco

Myanmar

Namibia

Nepal

New Zealand

Nicaragua

Pakistan

Panama

Copyright © 1994, Good Apple

72

GA1486

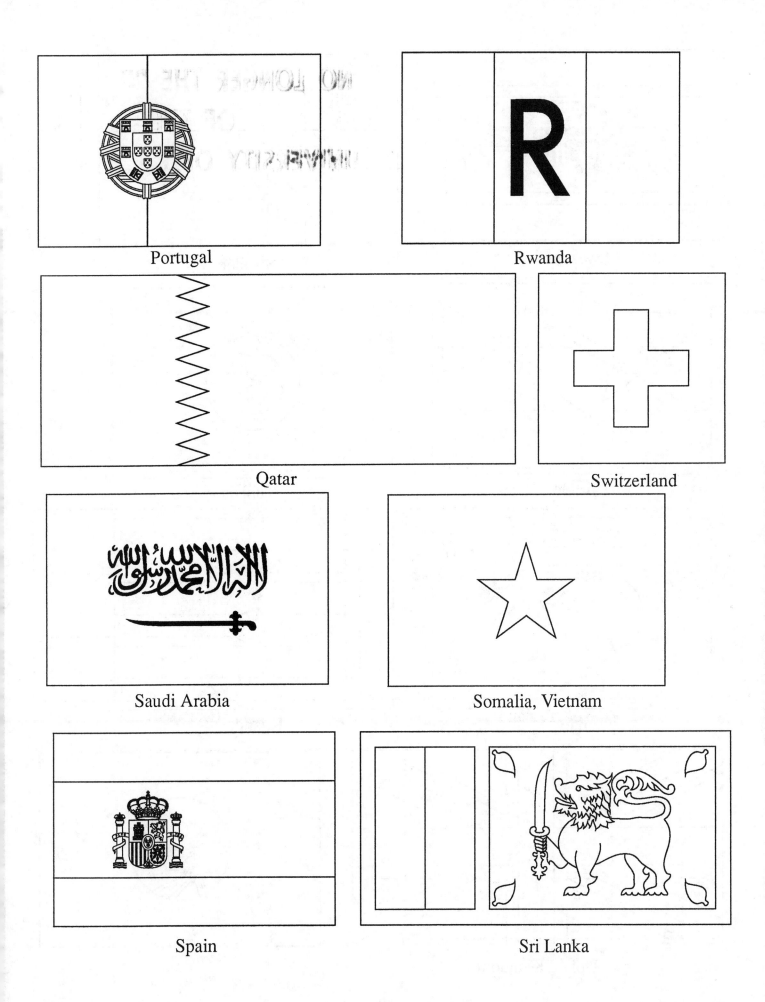

Portugal

Rwanda

Qatar

Switzerland

Saudi Arabia

Somalia, Vietnam

Spain

Sri Lanka

Copyright © 1994, Good Apple

73

GA1486

UNIVERSITY OF RHODE ISLAND

3 1222 01041 955 7

NO LONGER THE PROPERTY
OF THE
UNIVERSITY OF R.I. LIBRARY

Swaziland

Sweden

Syria

Tunisia

Turkey

Uganda

United Kingdom

Zaire

Copyright © 1994, Good Apple

GA1486